Instruments and Music

Woodwind

Daniel Nunn

Heinemann Library
Chicago, Illinois

www.heinemannraintree.com
Visit our website to find out
more information about
Heinemann-Raintree books.

To order:

☎ Phone 888-454-2279

💻 Visit www.heinemannraintree.com
to browse our catalog and order online.

Edited by Dan Nunn, Rebecca Rissman, and Sian Smith
Designed by Joanna Hinton-Malivoire
Picture research by Mica Brancic
Production by Victoria Fitzgerald
Originated by Capstone Global Library Ltd
Printed and bound in China by Leo Paper Products Ltd

15 14 13 12 11
10 9 8 7 6 5 4 3 2 1

Library of Congress Cataloging-in-Publication Data
Nunn, Daniel.
  Woodwind / Daniel Nunn.
     p. cm.—(Instruments and music)
  Includes bibliographical references and index.
  ISBN 978-1-4329-5063-7 (hc)—ISBN 978-1-4329-5070-5 (pb)
  1. Woodwind instruments—Juvenile literature. I. Title.
  ML931.N86 2012
  788.2′19—dc22   2010044785

Acknowledgments
We would like to thank the following for permission to reproduce
photographs: Alamy pp. 15 (© Lebrecht Music and Arts Photo
Library/Chris Stock), 16 (© Sue Cunningham Photographic); ©
Capstone Publishers pp. 21 (Karon Dubke), 22 (Karon Dubke);
Corbis pp. 13 (© Bob Krist), 20 (© Anders Ryman); Getty Images
p. 23 bottom (Comstock Images); Photolibrary pp. 4 (Polka Dot
Images), 7 (imagebroker.net/Wolfgang Diederich), 8 (Bluemoon
Stock/Harvey Edwards), 9 (Photos India RF), 10 (John Warburton-
Lee Photography/Christian Kober), 18 (Imagebroker.net/Heiner
Heine), 19 (Image Source), 23 middle (Image Source);
Shutterstock pp. 5 recorder (© Alexey Fursov), 5 flute (© Dragon_
Fang), 5 ocarina (© Ilya Rabkin), 5 panpipes (© Jiri Hera), 5 clarinet
(© Mikeledray), 5 bagpipe (© Slavoljub Pantelic), 6 (Chad
McDermott), 11 (© Ken Inness), 12 (© Ben Smith), 14 (© Tepic),
17 (Igor Normann), 23 top (Jack.Qi).

Cover photograph of a flute player in traditional Peruvian dress,
reproduced with permission of © Corbis (Bob Krist). Back cover
photograph of a woman playing a flute reproduced with
permission of Photolibrary (Bluemoon Stock/Harvey Edwards).

We would like to thank Jenny Johnson, Nancy Harris, Dee Reid,
and Diana Bentley for their assistance in the preparation of
this book.

Every effort has been made to contact copyright holders of
material reproduced in this book. Any omissions will be rectified in
subsequent printings if notice is given to the publisher.

Contents

Woodwind Instruments

recorder

tambourine

People play many instruments to make music.

People blow woodwind instruments.
Not all woodwind instruments are
made of wood.

reed

People play woodwind instruments by blowing on an edge or a reed.

keys

People play notes by covering holes or pressing keys.

Flutes

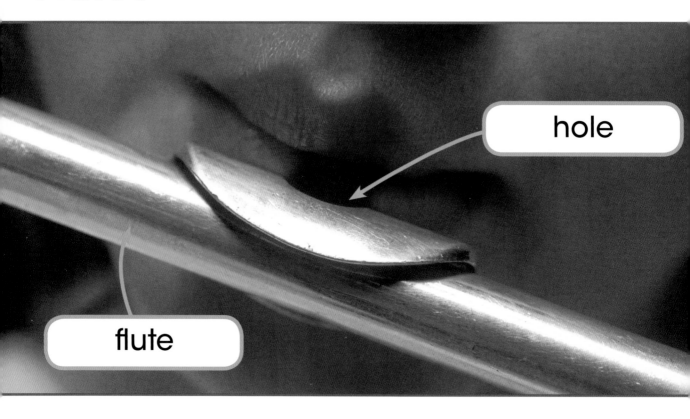

hole

flute

A flute makes a sound when people blow across the edge of a hole.

A nose flute makes a sound when people blow with their nose!

A dizi is a bamboo flute.

A piccolo is a small flute.

Reed Instruments

reed

A reed instrument makes sound when people blow against a reed.

The duduk is a very old reed instrument.

Bagpipes make sound when you squeeze a bag full of air!

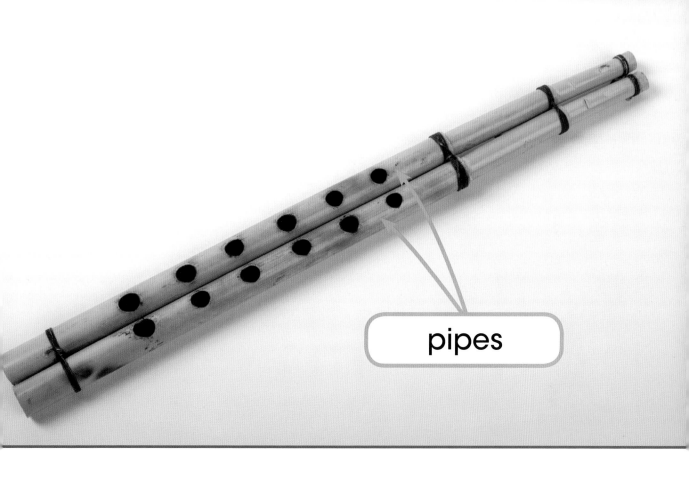

pipes

A mijwiz has two pipes instead
of one.

Playing Woodwind Instruments

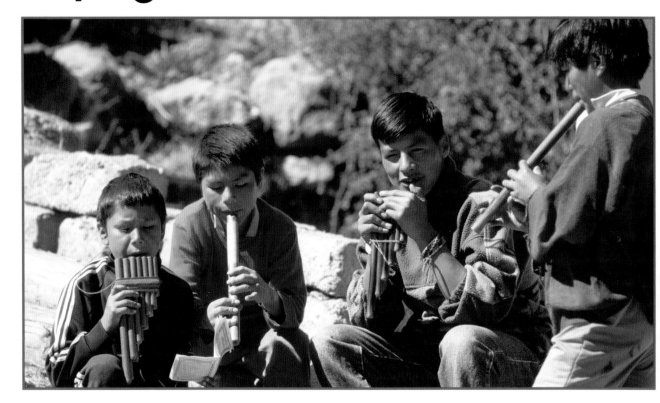

Some people play woodwind instruments together.

saxophone

Some people play woodwind instruments alone.

Some people play woodwind instruments for work.

Some people play woodwind instruments just for fun!

Making Woodwind Instruments

Some woodwind instruments are
hard to make.

Some woodwind instruments are easy to make.

Play Your Own Woodwind Instrument

You can play your own woodwind instruments, too!

Picture Glossary

 **bamboo** tall, woody grass with long, hollow stems

 **note** sound made by a musical instrument

 **reed** part of a woodwind instrument that moves when you blow on it to make a sound

Index

Notes for Parents and Teachers

Before reading
Show the children examples of woodwind instruments. Online examples with audio can be found at: http://www.sfskids.org/templates/instorchframe.asp?pageid=3. Can they name any of the instruments? How do they think the instruments are played? Demonstrate if possible. Show the children a reed. Explain that an instrument is in the woodwind group when it is played by blowing air against a reed or against a sharp edge.

After reading
Encourage the children to make their own woodwind instrument. Get them to fill some old glass bottles with water and blow over the tops to make different sounds. The more liquid in the bottle, the higher the sound (because there is less air to vibrate).

Extra information
The instruments shown on page 5 clockwise from the top are: recorder, flute, clarinet, panpipes, ocarina, and bagpipes.
The different types of woodwind instruments are: flute-type instruments, where the player blows over an edge to make a sound (e.g. recorder); single-reed instruments (e.g. saxophone); double-reed instruments (e.g. oboe); and vibrating-reed-in-a-frame instruments (e.g. harmonica).